Stand Up
for Yourself &
Your Friends

Dealing with Bullies & Bossiness
and Finding a Better Way

by Patti Kelley Criswell
illustrated by Angela Martini

Published by American Girl Publishing

16 17 18 19 20 21 22 23 LEO 10 9 8 7 6 5 4 3 2 1

Editorial Development: Darcie Johnston
Art Direction & Design: Jessica Rogers
Production: Jeannette Bailey, Virginia Gunderson, Laura Markowitz, Cynthia Stiles
Illustrations: Angela Martini
Special thanks to The Ophelia Project and to Jane Annunziata, PsyD

Library of Congress Cataloging-in-Publication Data
Criswell, Patti Kelley.
Stand up for yourself & your friends : dealing with bullies & bossiness and finding a better way / by Patti Kelley Criswell ; illustrated by Angela Martini.
pages   cm
Reprint, originally published in 2009.
ISBN 978-1-60958-738-3 (pbk.) — ISBN 978-1-60958-760-4 (ebook)
1. Bullying—Prevention—Juvenile literature. 2. Assertiveness in children—Juvenile literature. 3. Self-esteem in children—Juvenile literature. 4. Interpersonal conflict in children—Juvenile literature. 5. Interpersonal relations in children—Juvenile literature.
I. Martini, Angela, illustrator. II. Title. III. Title: Stand up for yourself and your friends.
BF637.B85C75 2016   302.34'3—dc23   2015020859

americangirl.com/service

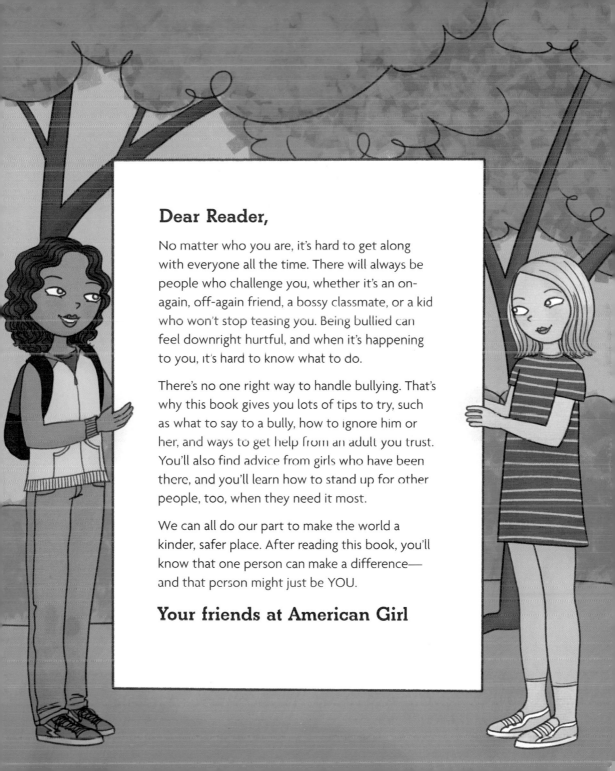

Dear Reader,

No matter who you are, it's hard to get along with everyone all the time. There will always be people who challenge you, whether it's an on-again, off-again friend, a bossy classmate, or a kid who won't stop teasing you. Being bullied can feel downright hurtful, and when it's happening to you, it's hard to know what to do.

There's no one right way to handle bullying. That's why this book gives you lots of tips to try, such as what to say to a bully, how to ignore him or her, and ways to get help from an adult you trust. You'll also find advice from girls who have been there, and you'll learn how to stand up for other people, too, when they need it most.

We can all do our part to make the world a kinder, safer place. After reading this book, you'll know that one person can make a difference— and that person might just be YOU.

Your friends at American Girl

Contents

Standing Up for Others 44

What's Bullying?

Teasing. Taunting. Being mean. No matter what you call it, one thing is for sure: It's all about power. People who bully are trying to take your power—the part of you that's strong, smart, and confident. They keep hurting your feelings with actions or words that are meant to be hurtful.

Is This Bullying?

Think you know what bullying is? Read about each situation, and decide whether or not it's bullying.

1. A boy in your class was sick and didn't make it to the bathroom in time. Now the kids call him a mean name. You don't call him that, but you laugh along.

Yes, it's bullying.
No, it's not.
I'm not sure.

2. It's the same thing day after day—you see the boys on the bus pushing and shoving as they try to get off the bus to go to school.

Yes, it's bullying.
No, it's not.
I'm not sure.

3. There is a girl in your class who is different. Lately people have been posting terrible things about her, but they never say anything to her face.

Yes, it's bullying.
No, it's not.
I'm not sure.

4. A girl comes up to you in the lunchroom and says, "I don't mean to be rude, but you need to move. Only my friends sit here."

Yes, it's bullying.
No, it's not.
I'm not sure.

5. One day she's your friend, and the next day she's sitting with someone else and won't talk to you.

Yes, it's bullying.
No, it's not.
I'm not sure.

6. A girl asks, "Can I play with you guys?" One of your friends says, "Sorry, it's not going to work out today."

Yes, it's bullying.
No, it's not.
I'm not sure.

7. You sometimes stumble over words when you read aloud. Every time it happens, the same girl corrects you.

Yes, it's bullying.
No, it's not.
I'm not sure.

8. You said something kind of mean to a classmate about his mom's car. You apologized afterward and tried to be extra nice to him the rest of the day.

Yes, it's bullying.
No, it's not.
I'm not sure.

1. **Yes.** Joining in the laughter means joining in the bullying. In fact, by encouraging the bullying, you may be doing as much harm as the bullies themselves.

2. **Maybe.** Are these boys just horsing around playfully, or is one or more of them trying to hurt or scare the others? Unwanted touching is definitely bullying. In a situation like this, talk to the bus driver or another trusted adult.

3. **Absolutely.** Gossiping—or talking behind someone's back—is one of the most hurtful forms of bullying. Using the Internet or devices such as smart phones to bully is called *cyberbullying,* and it's never OK. Not ever.

4. **Yes.** Saying "I don't mean to be rude" or "no offense" doesn't excuse mean behavior. This girl may think she's a leader, but bossing people around isn't leading—it's bullying.

5. **Yes.** Being an on-again, off-again friend is hurtful and not being a friend at all. If you've tried to talk to her and it keeps happening, you need a break. Let your friend know you need space, but be polite when you see her.

6. **Maybe.** If a group has made plans to spend time together outside of school, it's OK to say this in a polite way. And if someone has been treating you or your friends badly, you don't have to play with her. But if your friend is leaving this girl out to make her feel bad, then yes, that's bullying.

7. **Probably.** While this girl may be bragging about her own reading ability, she is embarrassing you in the process, and that's not OK. Ask her to please stop. If she doesn't, it's definitely bullying.

8. **No.** We all say stupid things once in a while. You let this boy know that you were sorry. It happened once, and you did your best to make it right. It was a mistake, not bullying.

What Does a Bully Look Like?

Bullies aren't all rough-and-tough looking. They can be girls or boys, kids or adults. Anyone can bully—even you. In fact, at one time or another, many of us will bully someone else. But whether we're teasing a sibling or purposely leaving out a friend, it's not OK. Here are some examples of bullying . . .

Gossiping or spreading rumors:

"Psst, did you hear about . . . ?"

Telling secrets:

"Don't tell her I told you, but . . ."

Name-calling:

"She's such a loser."

Pushing and shoving:

"Move!"

Excluding someone on purpose:

"You can't be in our club."

Embarrassing someone:

"Hey, everyone, watch this."

Teasing or putting someone down:

"I can't believe you don't know that!"

Scaring someone:

"You'd better do what I say."

Spot the Difference

The best way to tell if you're being bullied is simply by noticing how it feels. Bullying is done on purpose. It's usually done repeatedly, like a pattern. And it's meant to be hurtful. Being bullied feels bad.

**One says, "Sorry to bother you."
The other says, "Move it!"**

One is complimenting the shirt.
The other is making fun of it.

Bullying isn't always about the words you use. It's how you say them that can cause a person to feel bullied. Think about where your words are coming from and how your attitude might affect someone else. Watch your body language and tone of voice. Before you speak, use your head—and your heart.

Why People Bully

Why on earth would someone want to hurt someone else?
Good question. Maybe she . . .

★ is lonely.

★ has problems she doesn't know how to fix.

★ is jealous of other people's happiness.

★ is confusing being a leader with being a bully.

★ is angry.

★ is getting bullied at home, in her neighborhood, or somewhere else.

★ is trying to fit in.

★ needs more attention.

★ is sad.

★ is used to bullying others at home or elsewhere.

★ doesn't realize that being hurtful is wrong.

★ isn't very confident.

Any of these could be the reason a girl chooses to bully others. Most often, a bully doesn't feel good about herself deep down. But hurting others is not the way to feel better. In fact, being a bully makes a person feel worse, because at the end of the day, a person who bullies others can't really be proud of the person she is.

If you're bullied, it might help to know that the bully's reasons have nothing to do with you—it's not your fault. But it's important to remember this: Even if she's hurting inside, no reason ever makes bullying OK.

One thing is for sure . . .

Bullying Hurts!

Take it from real girls who know.

When this boy in my class tries to shock me with scary talk, I feel upset inside. Sometimes it makes me sick to my stomach, and I have to leave class. It makes me feel like I have no strength. Then I just feel bad about myself.

A girl on my bus keeps teasing me. Yesterday she called my name, and when I turned around, she made a face at me and smiled a satisfied smile. Everyone around her laughed and smiled, too. When I got off the bus, I was so angry! I cried all the way home and I felt like I was all alone.

Standing Up for Yourself

There's no one "right" way to deal with bullying. What may feel right for one person may not for someone else, and what works in one situation may not in another. What's important is that you look at what's happening, what you've tried so far, and what your options are. Then figure out a plan and decide who can help you along the way.

Just Ignore It

Many times girls are told to just ignore a bully. True enough, sometimes ignoring works. Other times, it doesn't, and the bullying continues. Ignoring the bully works best if you follow these tips.

★ Look the part

When you're ignoring a bully, do your best to look neutral or matter-of-fact, or even bored or annoyed—anything but scared or hurt. The bully is trying to upset you, so don't show that it's working. Practice your best neutral face at home, in front of a mirror.

★ Walk away

If you don't need to stay, walk away. You don't have to say a word. Just hold your head high, wear your neutral face, and calmly put one foot in front of the other.

★ Distract yourself

It's a lot easier to ignore a bully if you can pay attention to someone or something else. Find that person to talk with or that thing to do.

★ Think fast

If ignoring is going to work, it will work fast. If you have tried ignoring and the bullying continues for several days or more, chances are you need a new plan.

★ Assess your stress

Are you thinking about the bullying all the time? If ignoring a bully is affecting your happiness most days, causing you to feel sad or worried, it's time to try another strategy. Remember: You're not in the wrong here, and it's absolutely OK to stand up for yourself. Ignoring a bully is one option, but there are many others you can try.

23

How to Speak Up

Girls have lots of reasons for not standing up for themselves, but staying quiet doesn't always work. On the other hand, getting in someone's face or talking behind her back isn't the answer either. There's a better way.

It's called being *assertive*, which means speaking up with confidence, honesty, and respect for others. It's kind of the halfway point between being a pushover and being a bully. Here's how it works: You let the person know that you are not OK with the bullying, and you do it in a way that isn't mean and doesn't keep a fight going.

Will one of these work for you?
Practice a few smart strategies at home so that you'll be able to stand up for yourself when you need to.

★ **Tell it like it is.**
"I don't like it when . . ."

★ **Simply disagree.**
"I don't think so."

★ **Act surprised.**
"I can't believe
you said that!"

★ **Let her have her
point of view.**
"That's your opinion."

★ **Ask a question.**
"Was that really
necessary?"

★ **Use the one-word
technique.**
"Wow." or "Really."
or "Whatever."

★ **Question what she said.**
"That doesn't make sense."

★ **Just chuckle and
walk away.**
"That's pretty funny . . ."

★ **Act confused.**
"What? I don't know
what you're talking about."

★ **Say her name.**
"Monica!"

BIG
IMPORTANT POINT

None of these strategies contain words that can get you into trouble with grown-ups. You have a right to defend yourself, and there are smart ways to do it. Just be sure you speak up in a way that solves problems and doesn't create more for you.

What's Your Speak-Up Style?

Do you stand up for yourself? How? Read each question, and decide which response sounds most like you.

1. A girl in your class tells all the girls except one to wear pink on Wednesday. You . . .

   a. feel bad for the girl who was left out, but you mind your own business.

   b. decide that you don't want to be a part of hurting someone's feelings. You skip the pink.

   c. secretly try to convince the girls to wear purple instead. That way the rule maker will feel left out.

2. A girl on the playground asks you a personal question. You don't trust her. You respond by saying . . .

   a. "I dunno," and make a quick exit.

   b. "I'm not sure why you're asking me this. It's pretty personal."

   c. "That's none of your business. I wouldn't tell you even if we were friends."

3. While you're waiting in the lunch line, a classmate comes up, gives you a dirty look, and cuts in front of you. You . . .

   a. do nothing. It's not worth it.

   b. say, "Next time, please ask me and I'll let you in."

   c. say, "Hey, jerk! What do you think you're doing?!"

5. A boy trips and drops his lunch tray. You try to help, and a girl grabs your arm and tells you not to. You . . .

   a. stay seated, but you give the boy a kind look.

   b. pull your arm away and say to her, "I want to help him."

   c. say to her, "What's your problem? You're so mean!"

4. Every Friday is popcorn day at school. A girl in your class always expects you to give her money so that she can get a bag of popcorn. You say . . .

   a. nothing. After all, you started this by sharing with her in the first place, and you don't want to hurt her feelings.

   b. "I wanted to give you the heads-up that I don't have extra money this week."

   c. "I'm tired of you using me. Don't you have your own money?"

6. Some kids on the bus are picking on a boy from your neighborhood. You . . .

a. feel bad for him and give him a smile when he passes by.

b. invite him to sit with you.

c. stand up and say, "Knock it off, you guys. Just because you're flunking out doesn't mean you have to pick on the smart kid!"

7. Puppies are your absolute most favorite thing in the world. Everyone knows it. One day, a girl in your class forms a puppy club, but she says you can't join. You . . .

a. shrug your shoulders and find someone else to play with.

b. say, "That's too bad. It would have been fun to get all the puppy lovers together. But there's room for another puppy lovers group."

c. say, "No problem. I'll start my own club and invite everyone but you."

8. Two girls in your class are looking at you, whispering and giggling. You know they are making fun of you. You . . .

a. show them how hurt you feel, but you say nothing.

b. raise your eyebrows and say confidently, "C'mon, guys. Is that necessary?"

c. walk right up to them and say, "What's the matter? Are you too scared to say that to my face?"

Mostly a's

You try to steer clear of trouble, and you don't sweat the small stuff, even if it means not getting the things you want. Sometimes your easy, breezy style works well for you. Other times, you end up feeling like a doormat because you let people walk all over you. Finding your voice and letting others know how you feel is your challenge. Turn the page for tips from girls who found ways to be heard.

Mostly b's

You know how to stand up for yourself while also considering the feelings of others around you. Many people will admire the honesty and kindness you bring to problem solving. It's not always easy, but doing the right thing makes you a role model—and a good friend.

Mostly c's

You have no trouble telling people how you feel, and nobody is going to stomp on you—that's for sure. Trouble is, you may be pushing people away. Being mean in response to bullying just keeps the fight going. Work on standing up for yourself in a way that respects other people's feelings, too.

Words That Work

Need more inspiration to speak up? Try these tips from girls like you.

Whenever someone says something mean to me, I say, "Are you having a bad day?" That person really must be having a bad day to say something so mean to someone who hasn't done anything to her.

I say, "Oh, well!" If that's the way they want to be, let them be that way. It's their problem.

I just say, "Whatever," and I get away from them.

If someone insults what I'm wearing, I don't respond to that. Instead I say, "Hmmm, interesting" or "Whoa, that was harsh!"

I'm ready with a joke I've practiced. If I'm funny, it lets them know they can't hurt me, and the bullying usually stops.

I just say, "Thanks, but I'm good," and then I walk away.

BIG IMPORTANT POINT

If someone insults you, try not to defend or even acknowledge the insult itself. Instead, respond to the act of being insulted. So if a bully says, "That's an ugly shirt," instead of sticking up for the shirt, try saying something like, "Wow, that's pretty rude."

Staying Strong at School

Being bullied or bossed around at school is the worst. How can you concentrate when you're being picked on? Kids who bully are looking for a reaction. If you look upset, you'll be giving them the reaction they want. Instead, follow these tips to look strong and stand tall.

Act confident

Hold your head high and your shoulders back. Look the person in the eye, and try to keep your voice steady while you're talking. *Acting* confident will help you *feel* more confident.

Keep it cool

Try to look neutral, bored, or distracted. Don't let the bully know she's gotten to you.

★ Don't make threats to a bully. That rarely works.

★ Don't try to get even. Two wrongs don't make a right.

★ Don't ask others to take sides. It will just keep the fight going.

★ Don't stay home from school to avoid the bully. It doesn't solve the problem, and you create a new one by falling behind at school.

★ Don't yell, whine, or lose control. Bullies really feed on that!

Take a break

If you feel your confidence fading, step away from the situation and give yourself a pep talk. You can also turn to your friends or a favorite teacher when you need encouragement.

Breathe

Take a few long, deep breaths. Breathe in confidence and strength, and breathe out your stress and worry.

Splash!

If you feel as if your insides are on fire, cool down with a large drink of water. Or splash water on your face to help calm those hot feelings.

Assemble your allies

There's safety and power in numbers. Try to have a friend or two with you when you think a bully is likely to bother you.

Let it out

Think about an adult at school who can listen and help if you're having a tough day. If you don't have someone at school, write your feelings down so that you can talk about them when you get home.

What If It's Not Working?

You've tried ignoring the bully and you've tried standing up for yourself, but the bully isn't backing down. If this is happening to you, take heart. It's not easy to stand strong, but there *is* another option right around the corner.

Step 1: Reach out

Many girls feel embarrassed about being bullied. Just remember that it's NOT your fault. If you've tried speaking up and that's not working, get help from a parent or another adult you trust. Talk about what you have tried so far, and come up with a new plan that you're both comfortable with.

Step 2: Keep track

Start writing down when and where the bullying happens. Add a note about how you handle the bullying, too, for each incident that you record.

Step 3: Heads up!

Let your teachers in on what's up and what you have tried so far. They can keep an eye out for the bullying and maybe catch it while it's happening.

Step 4: Give a warning

Say firmly, "Leave me alone" or "This is bullying and you need to stop." That's enough to send the message that you mean business. Caution: If the bullying is severe and you feel unsafe, don't wait. Go straight to Step 5.

Step 5: Enough is enough

If you've kept track of the bullying, and you've told the bully to stop but the bullying continues, it's time to make a full report to the teacher or principal. Ask your parents to go with you, and take the notes that you've written.

BIG IMPORTANT POINT

You may worry that the bullying will get worse if you report it. Bullies often threaten, "You'd better not tell . . . " But people at school have experience with bullying and should know how to make it stop without causing more problems for you. Together with your parents, talk with the school about their plan and how you will be protected. And remember: Reporting should help the problem get better—for you and for anyone else who might be getting hurt. You'll feel stronger and more in charge, knowing you made a difference.

Getting Support

Now is the time to take extra care of yourself and to feel the support of those closest to you. Remember: A bully is trying to take your power. Hang on to it by reaching out to your family and doing things that make you feel strong, confident, and loved.

Keep talking

Talk regularly to your parents about what's happening. Set aside time to share your feelings, and work together to find a solution. You don't need to go through this alone.

Show team spirit

Your siblings can help, too. Hold a family meeting and brainstorm ways for you to deal with the bully. Role-play, or act out, different responses. If you're the oldest, you'll be teaching your siblings how to stand up for themselves. If you have older siblings who have been there, you can learn from their experiences.

Pour on the fun

When school is stressful, life at home can be a place to relax and recharge. Plan fun things during your free time. Cook or bake, have a family game night, read a great book, watch an inspiring movie, take a bubble bath, write in your journal, or call a faraway relative or friend. Try lots of different ways to lift your spirits.

Powerful Reminders

A *motto* is a positive saying that reminds you of who you are and what you are about. When you repeat your motto to yourself, negative feelings fade away and you grow stronger. It doesn't matter what anyone else says about you, because you know better. These tokens will remind you of your motto when you need it most. Use them when the bully comes near—and any time you feel discouraged.

Beads of bravery

Make a bracelet or key chain out of beads that spell out the first letter of each word in your motto. If your motto is "I'm strong, smart, and totally amazing," string beads with the letters I, S, S, T, and A. Wear the bracelet or tuck it into your pocket. When you see the bully coming or feel the sadness that comes with being bullied, think of the motto and touch the beads to give yourself strength and confidence.

Daily doodles

Write the initials of your motto on your notebook cover, on a postcard that you stick in your locker, or on a scrap of paper that you tuck into your pocket.

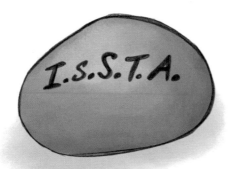

Solid as a rock

Use a permanent marker to write the initials of your motto on a small, smooth rock. Carry the rock with you throughout the day, and touch, hold, or rub it whenever you feel stressed or worried.

Colorful clothing

Does the color red make you feel strong? Then layer it on. Wear a red T-shirt on the days you need extra courage, or give yourself small bursts of bravery with a red headband, a bracelet, or painted toenails.

Feel-good music

Find the songs that speak to you, and put them in a playlist or on a music device. When you don't have your music with you, hum a few lines of a song in your head until you feel better.

Box of inspiration

Decorate a shoe box and fill it with notes, poems, quotes, and photos that make you feel strong and good about who you are. Keep adding to the box, and pull it out when you need a boost.

Token of esteem

Keep a small object in your pocket that has special meaning for you. Maybe it's a piece of sea glass from a favorite vacation or a basketball charm from your team. Whatever it is, it gives you a sense of strength or comfort.

What Do You Do?

The lunch supervisor at school seems to have something against you. She makes comments on what you pack, how fast you eat, and even how you laugh! You don't know why she doesn't like you, but it's clear she doesn't, and it's getting harder every day.

Whenever you're around Mimi, the queen bee in your class, you say something to annoy her, and she ends up humiliating you in front of her friends. You know she always acts this way, but you keep trying to talk to her. How can you slow down and stop yourself?

It's true—adults can bully, too. And being bullied by an adult can be especially painful and confusing. Whether that bully is a troop leader, a teacher, or a coach, you need to ask for help from another adult you trust. This takes a LOT of courage. Write down what is happening at lunch, and keep talking with another adult about how best to handle the situation. Remember that no one deserves to be bullied, whether by a kid or by an adult.

Maybe you talk because you're nervous, maybe you're trying to stick up for yourself because Mimi has hurt your feelings, or maybe it even seems cool at the moment to be talking with the queen bee. In any case, talking just fuels her fire. It may be best to try to avoid her altogether. If you feel the urge to say something when you're around her, write it down first. If you see it in writing, you'll have time to think about the best person to share it with. And that's clearly not Mimi.

You're chatting with Martina on your favorite website, and she starts saying mean things—really mean things—about Sarah. You can't believe what you're reading, and you're not sure what to do. Is this bullying?

You bet. *Cyberbullying*—using the Internet or a device to embarrass or hurt someone—is serious. If a friend starts bad-mouthing another friend online, you have options. You can say "gotta go" and log off. You can change the subject and hope she gets the hint. Or you can tell your friend straight up, "I don't want to hear or read mean things about Sarah. She's my friend, just like you. I would never let someone talk about you that way." If you ever receive a mean message directed at YOU, don't respond. Log off, and let your parents know right away. They can help you decide how to handle the situation. And when you're writing a message to someone, always think before pressing the "send" button, especially if you're angry. Once you put something in writing, you can't take it back.

Girls Who Stood Strong

If you are being bullied, you're not alone.
Many girls have gone through the same thing.

My bully troubles started in fifth grade at a new school. A girl started teasing me. She spread terrible rumors about me. She made fun of my body and my clothing, too. I tried to do what my family said and just ignore her, but I couldn't take it. I waited for a time when lots of teachers were around, and then I said straight to her face, "Stop saying mean things that aren't true! If you want me to go to the teachers, you can just keep spreading rumors!" She gave me nasty looks for the rest of the year, but I didn't care. At least she stopped making up things about me.

My friend Brittany would be nice some days and mean other days. I started to get stomachaches and couldn't sleep because I was worried about whether she'd ever be my friend again. I finally learned that if Brittany wanted to be mean, I would have to pull away and open up to other girls — nicer and stronger girls. I learned that you can control your own life.

There was a boy in my class who used to say awful things to me. He would say anything to get me upset, and it got so bad that I didn't want to go to school. I would get sick a lot and couldn't get my work done. I was very unhappy. My mom and I let the teacher know, and she tried to help by watching what was happening. She also checked in with me, which helped a lot. Then I stood up to him by making a joke and pretending I didn't care what he said. I felt much stronger after that, so I did it a few more times, and eventually he left me alone.

When you see someone being bullied, you have an important choice to make. You can stand aside and watch, or you can stand up for that person. If you stand up for her, you'll feel good—and you might add to the list of people who will be there for you if you ever need them.

Being a Good Ally

A person who sees someone else being bullied is called a *bystander*. Good bystanders—the ones who do something to help the person being bullied—are called *allies*. One way to be an ally is to say out loud to the bully that you don't agree with her and you want her to stop. Can't find the words? Practice a few of these.

C'mon, let's get out of here!

Telling or Tattling?

Another way to be an ally is to report what is happening to an adult. Afraid of being a tattletale? You won't be. There's a HUGE difference between telling and tattling. Knowing the difference will give you the courage and confidence to report bullying when you see it.

Tattling

You're trying to make someone look bad. The goal is not to help someone but to get someone into trouble.

Telling

You're reporting a behavior that is hurting you or someone else. It's something you feel adults should know about, and you are trying to help someone. Chances are, you're not the only one who doesn't like what's going on. If you speak up, others may, too.

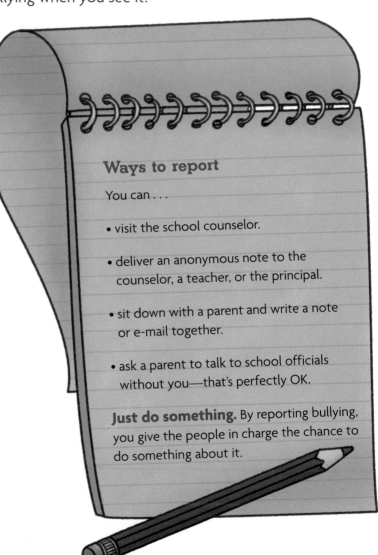

Ways to report

You can . . .

• visit the school counselor.

• deliver an anonymous note to the counselor, a teacher, or the principal.

• sit down with a parent and write a note or e-mail together.

• ask a parent to talk to school officials without you—that's perfectly OK.

Just do something. By reporting bullying, you give the people in charge the chance to do something about it.

49

Girls Who Stood Up for Others

Here's how other girls found the courage to be allies.

Once I heard a boy in my class make really rude comments to a girl on the playground. The girl looked upset by what he was saying, and I knew it was wrong but wasn't sure what to do. That night, I told my mom. She said I was right to tell her, and together we wrote an e-mail to the teacher. No one ever knew that I was the one who stood up for that girl, but I knew, and it made me feel really good.

There is a kid who said really bad things to my friends. I stood up for them by saying, "Ewww, that's gross! Keep your thoughts to yourself." I'm not sure if he got into trouble, but he hasn't done it since. If he does it again, I'll report it, because that's just wrong.

Last year, my three new "friends" were ganging up on one girl who had a problem with her speech. I felt horrible, but it was REALLY hard to go against my friends. But I asked myself, "If they are pressuring me to do things I don't want to do, are they really my friends?" The answer is no. If they threaten to take away their friendship, their friendship isn't worth that much. Being nice to someone who is being bullied gives you confidence in yourself—and more power than any bully has.

One day my friends were being really mean to a girl who gets picked on, and I joined in. When I got home I felt really bad, so I called the girl and told her I was sorry. She really appreciated that I called her. Now when kids are teasing her, I stand up for her. Once I started standing up for this girl, many other girls started doing the same.

Caring for Friends

Speaking up isn't always easy, and sometimes the chance to be an ally passes you by. But it's never too late to let a friend know you're in her corner.

Say what you think
Say, "They're wrong," or "They're bullies. Don't listen to them." Try, "I think you're a great person," "That was not cool," or simply "Hang in there."

Send her a note
A little bit of kindness can go a long way. Write, "Sending a smile your way" or "Ten things I like about you."

Help her reach out
Offer to go with her to report what is happening, or encourage her to talk to an adult.

Make a wish
Tell her what you wish could've happened or what you wish you had said or done.

Reassure her
Let your friend know you won't take part in any gossip behind her back. Tell her you would never do that—and then don't.

Stay close
Give her a hug, sit by her at lunch, and stand by her in gym. Just having you close will mean a lot.

Give her a break
Call her, tell her a joke, or make plans to get together outside of school. Don't waste your time talking about the negative stuff at school. Instead, focus on having fun.

What Do You Stand For?

It's easier to stand up for yourself and others when you know what you believe. Read each statement below and decide whether you agree or disagree.

1. One student like me can't really make my school a better place.

agree   **disagree**

2. I think it's important to make everyone happy. I don't want anyone to be mad at me.

agree   **disagree**

3. When someone makes me angry, it's OK for me to be mean.

agree   **disagree**

4. It's easiest to go along with my friends, even when something they're doing doesn't feel quite right.

agree   **disagree**

5. People who act "different" are sort of asking to be bullied.

agree   **disagree**

6. If I'm upset with a friend, it's probably time to end the friendship.

agree   **disagree**

Did you "disagree" most often? If so, you know how to stand up for your beliefs—and how to respect other people's points of view. It's not easy to do both. These tips should help:

1. The principal isn't the only one with power at your school. Every time you give a kind smile or help someone out, you make your school a better place. One person can make a difference, and you're just the one to do it.

2. It's impossible to keep everyone happy, and it's exhausting to even try. Instead of worrying about others getting angry, focus on the respect you'll get when you speak up and how proud you'll be when you stay true to yourself.

3. It's OK to be angry. What's not OK is expressing it in mean ways. Being mean almost always makes things worse. Next time you feel angry, slow down and think about why you feel that way. Then figure out the best way to deal with it.

4. It may seem easiest to give in to peer pressure. But you have to live with your decisions, and there's nothing easy about knowing that you did something you knew was wrong. Listen to the voice inside of you *before* doing something you'll regret.

5. No one should be bullied for being different. No two people are alike anyway, and everyone has the right to be who they are. Stand up for those who dare to be different, because it's the right thing to do. Also, the world would be a boring place without them!

6. Nobody's perfect. You're not, and your friends aren't either. Making mistakes is part of being human, so try to give friends a chance to make things right. But if a friend keeps doing things that are hurtful, it's time to set some limits.

Changing Friendships

Does standing up for what you believe sometimes mean clashing with friends? Absolutely. Friends can disagree—that's OK. But if it seems as though you just can't get along, take time to figure out why.

Talk to your friend

If you think a friendship is worth fighting for, have a heart-to-heart talk with your friend. Tell her how you are feeling, and then decide if you can work things out. You may have to agree to disagree on some things.

Stay open

Part of growing up is making mistakes (and forgiving them). Never be too proud to apologize or too stubborn to accept an apology.

Watch and wait

Maybe there is something going on with your friend, or maybe she's just trying on different roles. Put off making big decisions and see what happens. This problem may be temporary.

Focus on other friends

If you and your friend are moving in different directions, that's normal. You can still be friends. You just might spend less time together. Be friendly and kind, and put energy into other relationships that allow you to be YOU.

BIG
IMPORTANT POINT

Not all friendships last a lifetime. While some get even better over time, others slip away. Changing friendships allow you to change and grow, too.

What Do You Do?

You made a mistake. You shared a secret that you shouldn't have, and now your friend Cierra can barely look at you. You've really hurt her feelings, and you feel terrible. What do you do?

You try to make it right. Admitting you were wrong isn't easy. But taking responsibility for your mistakes is the first step toward healing the damage. Apologize to Cierra. Tell her what you wish you had done and what you'll do differently in the future. Be sensitive, and be patient. In time, she may forgive you. If she doesn't, you'll know you've done all you can—and learned a difficult lesson about the importance of trust in a friendship.

Melani used to make fun of you in second grade. In fact, you still get a sick feeling in your stomach when you think about it. Now she wants to be your friend. Can you ever forgive her?

If you believe she is truly sorry for hurting you and wants to be friends, then you may want to give it a try. That doesn't mean you have to be close friends right away, or ever. Just give her a chance to earn back your respect and friendship. Take it slowly. Don't accept the best-friends necklace from Melani just yet, and wait before doing an overnight or spending lots of one-on-one time with her. After a while you'll know if you can be good friends or if you're better off as casual pals.

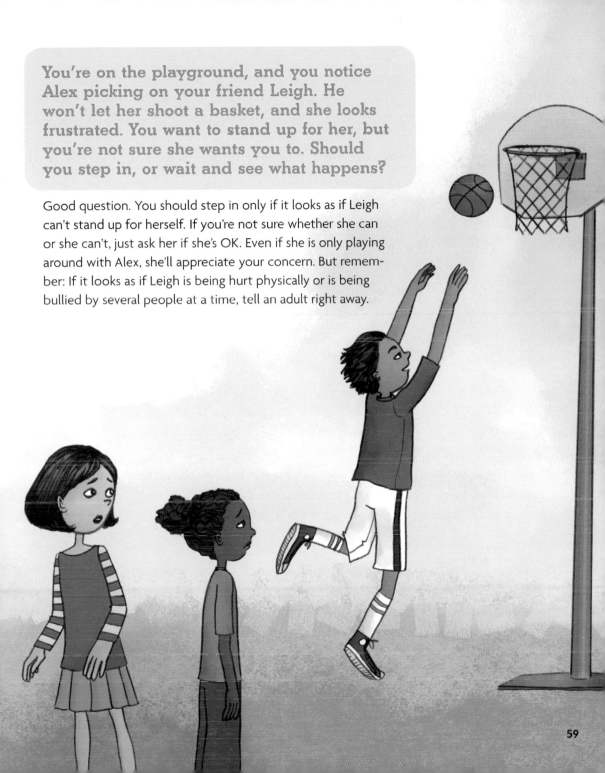

You're on the playground, and you notice Alex picking on your friend Leigh. He won't let her shoot a basket, and she looks frustrated. You want to stand up for her, but you're not sure she wants you to. Should you step in, or wait and see what happens?

Good question. You should step in only if it looks as if Leigh can't stand up for herself. If you're not sure whether she can or she can't, just ask her if she's OK. Even if she is only playing around with Alex, she'll appreciate your concern. But remember: If it looks as if Leigh is being hurt physically or is being bullied by several people at a time, tell an adult right away.

Shining Bright

We all have an invisible spark inside us—call it our inner star. There are things we can do to make our stars shine, and one of them is to be kind to others. When we do something kind, we not only help someone else's inner star to shine . . . we also polish up our own.

Whenever you can, help other people shine.

Stand up for them when they need it most.

Give a hug.

Give a warm smile.

Offer a compliment.

Make a Difference

We can all do our part to stop the bullying. You can stand up for yourself, your friends, and others around you. After reading this book, you know it takes strength, courage, and also a bit of skill. You also know you can do it. YOU can make a difference!